512
MAR   Marks, Jennifer L.

Sorting by color

34880060910432
23.93

DATE DUE	BORROWER'S NAME	ROOM NUMBER
	Karina	204
	Ashley	215
	Evelyn	
1-13		

512 MAR $13.74
Marks, Jennifer L.

Sorting by color /

34880060910432

CPS-Morrill School Library
6011 South Rockwell Street
CHICAGO, IL 60629

Sorting

SORTING BY Color

by Jennifer L. Marks

Capstone press®

Mankato, Minnesota

A+ Books are published by Capstone Press,
151 Good Counsel Drive, P.O. Box 669, Mankato, Minnesota 56002.
www.capstonepress.com

1 2 3 4 5 6 12 11 10 09 08 07

Library of Congress Cataloging-in-Publication Data
Marks, Jennifer L.
    Sorting by color / by Jennifer L. Marks.
    p. cm.—(A+ books. Sorting)
    Summary: "Simple text and color photographs introduce basic concepts of sorting by color"—Provided
by publisher.
    Includes bibliographical references and index.
    ISBN-13: 978-0-7368-6739-9 (hardcover)
    ISBN-10: 0-7368-6739-2 (hardcover)
    ISBN-13: 978-0-7368-7857-9 (softcover pbk.)
    ISBN-10: 0-7368-7857-2 (softcover pbk.)
    1. Group theory—Juvenile literature. 2. Colors—Juvenile literature. I. Title. II. Series.
QA174.5.M37 2007
512'.2—dc22   2006018205

Credits

Ted Williams, designer; Charlene Deyle, photo researcher; Scott Thoms, photo editor

Photo Credits

Capstone Press/Karon Dubke, cover, 3, 4–5, 6–7, 8, 9, 10–11, 12, 13, 14–15, 16, 17, 18,
    19, 20, 21, 22, 23, 24, 25
Shutterstock/Arturo Limon, 29; David Yuckert, 26; Diego Cervo, 28; Sasha Davas,
    27 (paint swatches); V. J. Matthew, 27 (towels)

Note to Parents, Teachers, and Librarians

The Sorting set uses color photographs and a nonfiction format to introduce readers to the key
math skill of sorting. *Sorting by Color* is designed to be read aloud to a pre-reader, or to be read
independently by an early reader. Images and activities encourage mathematical thinking in early
readers and listeners. The book encourages further learning by including the following sections: Table
of Contents, Venn Diagram, Facts about Color, Glossary, Read More, Internet Sites, and Index. Early
readers may need assistance using these features.

The author dedicates this book to her sister Rachel Marks of Mankato, Minnesota.

Table of Contents

So Many Shoes!

Look at this jumble of colorful shoes! How can we sort them?

Let's sort these shoes by color. We can make blue, pink, tan, and purple sets. A set is a group of alike things.

What else can
we sort by color?

Sorting Food

A bag of fresh vegetables holds all kinds of crisp, tasty colors.

Let's sort them into sets—green, orange, yellow, and purple.

Yummy fruit can be sorted by color too. What three color sets do you see here?

Hungry for something even sweeter? Jellybeans are tiny but oh so tasty.

Sort these sweets
by color—red, orange,
yellow, green,
and blue.

Toys and Games

Toys can be sorted by color too. These huggable teddy bears are sorted— white, black, and brown.

Chinese checkers is a game that starts with sorting.

The pegs are sorted by color. After each player chooses a set, the fun begins.

Arts and Crafts

Let's sort crayons by color. We'll make sets of orange, yellow, green, and blue.

Why not sort your paints and brushes by color too?

It's lots of fun to press, pinch, and shape play dough into colorful creatures.

When you are done, sort the dough by color—green, yellow, and pink.

Venn Diagrams

Sometimes things can be sorted into more than one set. Let's use a Venn diagram to sort orange and blue shirts.

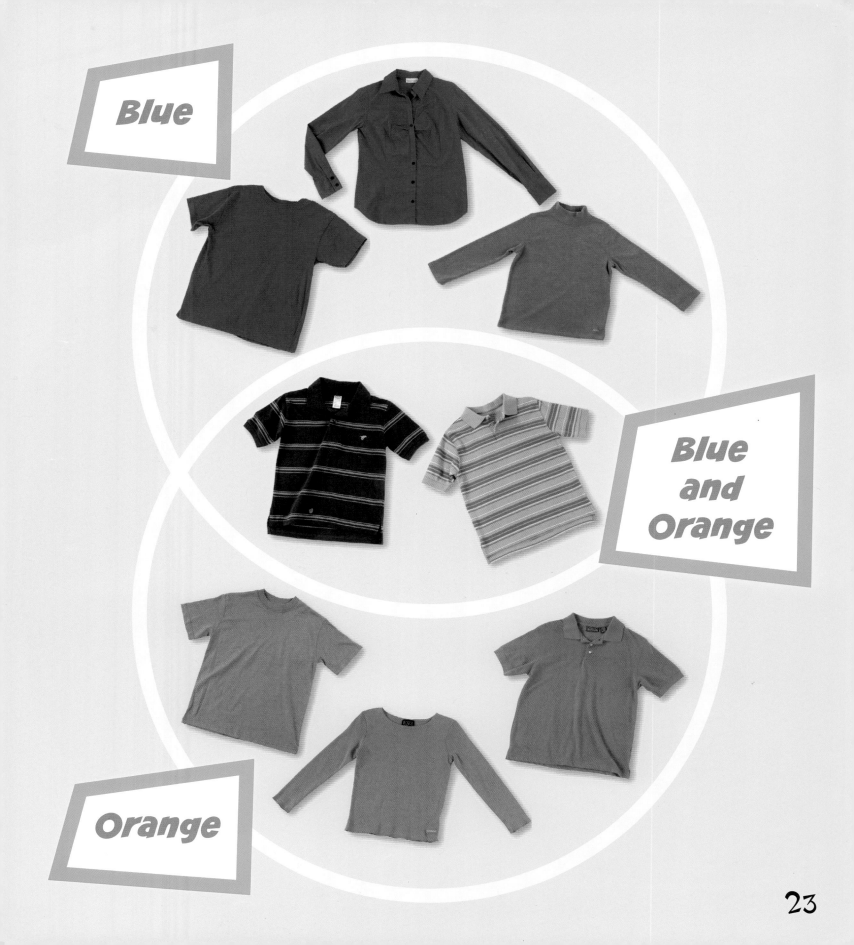

Blue

Blue and Orange

Orange

Fresh from the dryer, warm, fuzzy socks need to be sorted. Let's try another Venn diagram.

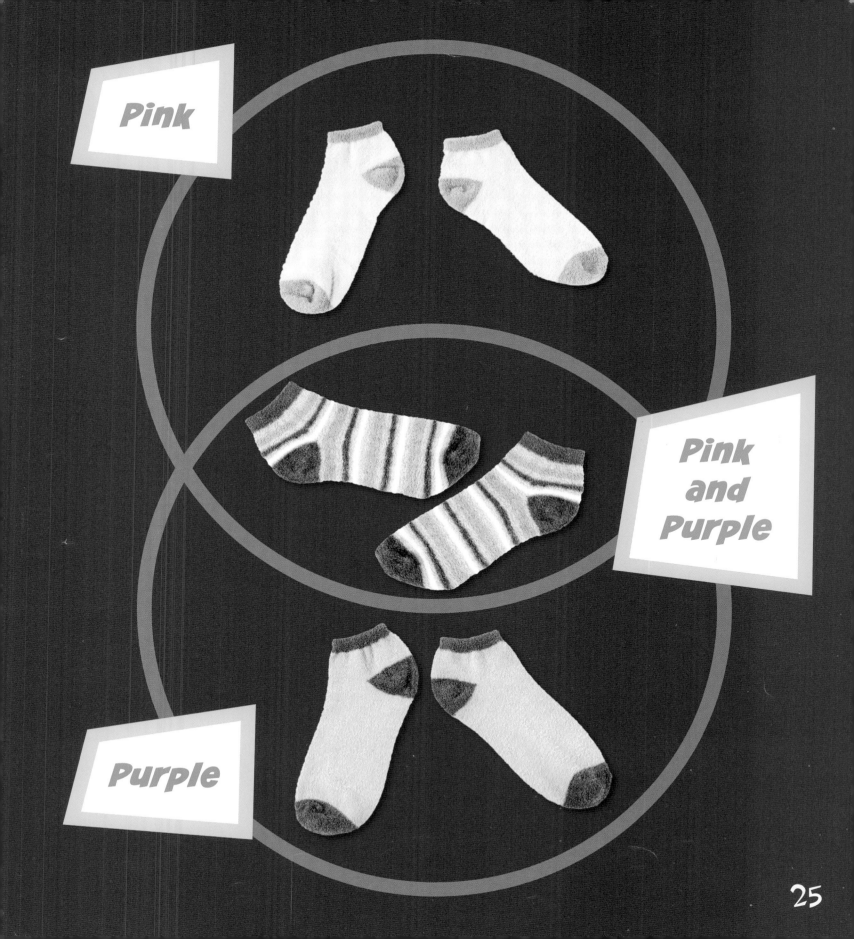

Pink

Pink
and
Purple

Purple

25

Sorting by Color in the Real World

You can spot sorting in all kinds of places. Let's look at some of the ways people sort by color in the real world.

Red, yellow, orange, and green peppers are sorted by color in a grocery store.

In department stores, towels are sorted by color. Shoppers can find just the color they need.

Stores that sell paint sort paint samples by color. The sorted samples make it easy for people to pick out the perfect color and shade of paint.

Facts about Color

- The first Crayola crayons came in eight colors—black, blue, brown, green, orange, red, violet, and yellow. Today, there are more than 100 colors of crayons. To celebrate Crayola's 100th anniversary, four new colors were added in 2003—inch worm, jazzberry jam, mango tango, and wild blue yonder.

- In grocery stores, you can see lots of potatoes sorted by color—red, white, yellow, even blue! The only potato color you should not eat is green. Green spots on potatoes can make you sick. Cooks cut off spots before the potatoes are cooked.

- Toothbrush companies, dentists, and the Massachusetts Dental Society all report that blue is the most popular toothbrush color in the United States.

- What happens if you decide not to sort your play dough by color? You can make new colors by squishing two colors together. Mix red and blue to make purple. Or mush yellow and red together to make orange. What color might you get if you mix blue and yellow?

- A little extra color can make food look even more delicious. Some food colors are made in laboratories. Others come from natural sources. Beets are often used to give pink lemonade its rosy color.

Index